"This information was massi... shared in this book will DEFINITELY be used on our campus. I believe that with these marketing tools our student involvement with activities will massively increase."

- Ronesha Barnet, Kishwaukee College, IL

"Mike's infomration is VERY helpful. He taught me new ideas for our upcoming events that I have never thought of. His enthusiasm alone makes me want to implement this information."

- Ilhan Hussaini, Service Coordinator of Student Leadership Counsil, College of DuPage, IL

"We are going to completely recreate our marketing based upon Mike's information."

- Danny Atten, Illinois Math and Science Academy, IL

"Not only did Mike help my activities board increase it's event size, his ideas can be applied to almost everything in life."

- Joe Torress, Harper College, IL

"Great marketing tips to ensure the success of your events on campus."

- Austin Friedmeyer, Lincoln Land Community College, IL

"Mike's 3 phases of marketing were all ones that we didn't do and are starting to implement. Amazing information."

- Maggie Foss, Hawkeye Community College, IA

"I got more out of Mike's information than from any book in a long time. He knows what he is talking about."

- Amy Batura, Moraine Park, WI

"As a graphic artist, I realized that throwing events on your campus is more of a marketing exercise. If we want students to come we need to think like marketers."

**- Clarisa Carrol, Lone Star College
North Harris, Houston TX**

Mike's Book helped me reshape my view on campus event promotion altogether. Mike definitely knows what he's talking about when it comes to helping boost event attendance."

**- Dora M Cautu, University of the
Incarnate Word, San Antonio TX**

"This book transformed how we were doing our campus marketing into something phenomenal."

- Giovanni Lopez, University of Texas, Austin TX

"Mike is phenomenal. I have learned so many things from this amazing resource to implement into my school. He is a marketing genius."

- Chesney Spears, Texas A & M, College Station TX

"This is the best marketing content I have ever heard"

- Bernice Zuniga, UNT, TX

HOW TO DOUBLE AND EVEN TRIPLE THE SIZE OF
YOUR NEXT CAMPUS EVENT

THE ONLY EVENT PROMOTION BOOK YOU WILL EVER NEED FOR YOUR CAMPUS

Mike Fritz International:

*How to Double and even TRIPLE the
Size of Your Next Campus Event*

*The Only Event Promotion Book You will Ever
need for your Campus*

by Mike Fritz

HOW TO DOUBLE AND EVEN TRIPLE THE SIZE OF

YOUR NEXT CAMPUS EVENT

THE ONLY EVENT PROMOTION BOOK YOU WILL EVER NEED FOR YOUR CAMPUS

Mike Fritz

Mike Fritz

QUOTES FROM MIKE

*"You are the only YOU this word has,
don't rob us of Him/her."*

"Your decisions today will create your tomorrow?"

*"The greatest mistake teenagers make is living up
to the expectations others have for them, rather
then reaching for their greatest potential."*

"Leaders only have the limits they place on themselves."

"You are always one choice away from being a leader."

*"Being popular doesn't mean you will be a good leader, and
being a good leader doesn't mean you will be popular."*

*"You never become better by seeking
to live somebody else's life."*

*"Expectations are often our finish line. But make
no mistake, most people fall short of their ability
because expectations are set too low."*

Mike Is The Ideal Speaker For Your Next Event!

To Book Mike To Speak At Your Next Event:
Call 269-370-2858, visit www.mikefritz.net,
or email booking@mikefritz.net

About Mike

What do you get when you mix a standup comedian and someone who has a master's degree in leadership? One of the most sought after speakers on the college circuit. Mike's knowledge of leadership and the ability to make people laugh until it hurts is unmatched. Mike's program "Making Leadership F.U.N." is not only booked all over the country, but maintains a 92% rebooking rate. When people have this program to their campus they want it back! In just his 2nd year on the college circuit Mike was voted APCA National College Speaker of the year finalist and has authored of the bestselling books "Great Student Leaders Aren't Born They're Made" and "Making

Leadership F.U.N." Mike has been featured on Fox, NBC, ABC, Forbes and over 200 business journals speaking on the topic of student engagement. He has shared the stage with NFL QB and Superbowl champion Joe Thiesmann (also featured on the Hit Blockbuster movie "The Blindside"), Glenn Morshower (Aaron Pierce on The Hit TV show 24 also in Transformers along with many others), LA Clippers Asst. coach Kevin Eastman and many more! When you bring Mike's programs to your campus your students will laugh until it hurts, learn until they change and lead until they influence.

TABLE OF CONTENTS

10 TIPS FOR CHOOSING THE RIGHT SPEAKER/ENTERTAINER OR NOVELTY

20 TIPS TO DOUBLE AND EVEN TRIPLE THE SIZE OF YOUR NEXT CAMPUS EVENT

TIP #1:

When You Put on an Event...YOU ARE A MARKETER...PERIOD!!!

When you bring an event to your campus/school you are no longer only a Student Government Member or Member of Student Activities, you are a marketer of the events, services and products your student organization provides!!! This is quite possibly the most important fundamental truth you must understand to get people to come to your events!!!!

Marketing is the missing link to your events and the people you want to come. You have to understand that people will never attend an event they don't know about. Sounds stupid right? However, this statement represents one of the many lies students and event coordinators believe.

5 LIES PEOPLE BELIEVE WHEN THROWING AN EVENT:

1. *If you throw it they will come.* If they don't know about it they will never come; and even if they do, you have to prove to them that they can't live without this event.

2. *These students "need" this event.* While this may be true it doesn't matter what they need, it matters what they want. How many people "need" the size house they live in? Need and want are completely different things.

3. *Your event changes lives.* Some of you might fight me on this, but stop thinking these events change lives; instead understand events are to inspire people to change their own lives!

4. *If the comedian, musician, speaker, etc. is good enough people will show up.* This lie is tricky! There is an element of truth in it. However, if people don't know that this great speaker is coming to town they still won't come. Hiring a great speaker doesn't alleviate your need to market the event.

5. *A poster in the hall will put a butt in the seat.* Nothing could be further from the truth. A poster in the hall just means that the speaker on that poster will soon have one of those mustaches

and a funky goatee from creative student graffiti. Make sure you put posters around campus, but never...never...never rely on that solely.

Many organizations have wasted time, money and other resources on events that bombed because these lies were their beliefs about running events. I want to make sure all of the amazing events you guys put on get as many people to them as possible.

Market...market...and market some more. When you have done all the marketing you planned on doing, you are about 30% there. Many events that have amazing content and great talent never get to be experienced because people didn't know about the event.

When you are choosing an act for your event make sure they help a little bit with this. One of their concerns should be the success of your event; after all, that is why you are hiring them instead of someone else. One of the things I learned early on in my speaking career is the more I helped give the event coordinator ideas and materials to market the event, the better the event went. Now I send a packet of marketing materials to people who book me to speak so they can hang them all over and they don't have to create them.

I make it as easy as possible for the event coordinator because they are too busy to be worrying about things that should be a speakers area of expertise.

TIP #2:

The Bonus Technique!!!

I don't know if you have ever gone fishing, but fishing without bait would be extremely ineffective. And so it goes with your event! I have had great success with this tip...give away as many prizes as your budget allows. And give away the prizes for many different reasons - raffle, contests, tallest, have a cutest contest, etc. Think of reasons to give things away. And be sure you are giving away prizes that your audience will value. They don't have to necessarily be expensive.

Another trick I have used many times is to give the first 50 (or you choose the number) people through the door a free copy of the speaker's book or the band's CD or the Comedian's DVD, etc.! I have given away 2 free books to the first 50 and one free book to the next 50. You can usually work out a deal with the speaker or ask to get significant discounts for product if you have booked them to perform on your campus.

On a side note, going back to our fishing example, the more desirable the bait the more fish you will attract. The better the prize the more people you will attract! What is it that college students want that you could give them?

Another way to use the bonus technique is to make sure you have free food when people show up; again, this will depend on the size of your event! Americans and those who live in America love food...so give it to them! Often times you can partner with local business to cater your events if you hand out coupons to their restaurant (yet another gift for attending) to those who attend. Remember, the idea is simply to give "bonuses" or "rewards" to the students who come to your event.

We, as humans, like getting something for what we do. I know, it goes all the way back to getting a sticker in elementary for spelling your word correctly; that desire for a "gift" apparently doesn't leave when we get older!

Incentives work! I'll prove it to you. What does Sports Illustrated sell? Most of you would probably say magazines. That is actually incorrect. They sell bonuses. Often they will say, "If you buy a subscription you get a free football phone/swimsuit edition/1980's San Francisco 49er's highlights, etc." People buy the magazines because of the bonuses. Do you think if that didn't work they would still be using the bonus technique?

Your goal is to apply the bonus technique to your event. Get a gift that students would be stoked about and fits your budget, then give it to the first 100 attendees (or whatever numbers fits your situation).

I know this may seem basic, but you have to tell them this over all of your marketing materials. You might event put at the top of the event poster, "Want a FREE Ipad?" or "Need a new cell phone?" Then tell what they need to do to get it...i.e. come to your event!

TIP #3:

Extra Credit Rules!!!

One of the best ways to get students to an "extra" event is give extra credit to the students who show up! I know what your thinking (again…it's like I have some sort of creepy mind reading thing going on here), "I don't control that type of thing - the teachers do!"

This tip is more specific to an event where you have content being taught such as a speaker teaching on topics like career, leadership, diversity, drugs and alcohol, campus safety, dating, etc.

To do this, what you have to do is locate teachers who teach subjects that are closest to the content that is going to be presented and ask the professor if they would be willing to give students extra credit if they attend! There are two responses that usually come from professors when this proposition is made. The first is they are ecstatic that students are engaged in something like this and they are happy to offer extra credit. The second can be a negative response due to their concern that the content may not be "academic" and therefore not credible. This is a legitimate concern; due to the fact that if students are getting credit for things that really aren't academic and helpful it devalues the education, however, there are some hidden secrets you can use to limit the amount of times the second one happens! As you know, in every event you conduct you must seek to add value, make a difference and enrich people's lives.

Here are 5 words/phrases to NEVER use when you are talking to a professor seeking to get their support for an event...because it scares professors and makes them skeptical of giving credit for it. Remember, these are words that you don't use with professors...on your marketing however, you would use every one of them! Also, this isn't true of every professor, there are a few select ones who are fine with these words!

1. *"Event"* - don't use this word! Event portrays the idea of an experience rather than content. Replace with seminar. Seminar has been a word for a long time that has been used when content and principles are being taught.

2. *"Real-world strategies"* - this goes directly against the idea of academia. Replace with "text-book strategies." Profs are trained to think in terms of text books.

3. *"Experience"* - This word is far too subjective and is unclear if you are internalizing any content. Replace with the word "learn" or "simulate". For example, instead of "It will be a great experience for us," say "After looking at what he is going to be teaching we will have the opportunity to learn great content." BIG difference!

4. *"Fun"* - I know this sounds harsh, but your professors are not concerned about you having fun: They are concerned with you being educated; and for that we should all be thankful. But fun, to a professor, can mean the absence of content. This is NOT the case, but it doesn't matter; all that matters is how your prof perceives it! Instead of saying, "This event is going to be so fun", highlight what the speaker is going to teach. For example, "He is going to dissect and teach us how to be a leader."

5. *"Funny, Dynamic, Entertaining."* These words highlight HOW the speaker presents not WHAT the speaker presents. You ALWAYS want to highlight the WHAT not the HOW when addressing your profs!

The content I just gave you is worth the entire investment you made in this book! I say that because there are few things that will get more people to your event than giving them extra credit. This is a sure fire way to increase your event involvement.

If you notice I am not taking time to convince you to do this...this concept is a gold mine for event involvement. I am going to spend most of our time on the how, not the why!

There are a couple of things to ALWAYS include in the conversation with your professor when asking him/her to offer extra credit for event attendance. One thing you need to understand is that professors think in terms of "learning objectives." When you are negotiating with a speaker ask them to send 5 learning objectives of their presentation. Take them with you, typed and printed out, when you talk to the professor. The more prepared you look when you go and talk to them, the more the professor feels like this is a legitimate investment of their classroom-credit.

The second thing is to highlight the book that the speaker has written. After reading my section on "NEVER book a speaker who hasn't written a book," I know you would NEVER do that!!! But seriously professors think in terms of text books. Books are the key to present and continued learning. How many times do you need to buy DVD's or audios at the beginning of the semester? Maybe every now and then, but most of the time it is books! Authors have more respect and are esteemed higher by educators. Play that card heavily!!!!

TIP #4:

Who is Bringing Whom?

People draw people!!!! Have you ever gone to something that you didn't really care much about but your friend was going so you agreed to it? I have done this many times. We aren't going to an event, we are spending time together at an event! This is the culture you want to set up. One practical way to cultivate this is to have a contest to see who can bring the most people. Then give a gift to the person who wins the contest!

I would limit the number of people you allow in the contest to encourage early sign up. So now you have a signup (online and a hard copy signup and update it often) and the first 20 people to sign up get to compete for the gift (iPad, Kindle Fire, spaceship, new car…okay I was just kidding about the spaceship).

When people show up to the event, have them fill out an attendance form. Information on this would include: how they heard about the event (that way you can track what is working and do more of it), if they came with someone and who it was, their most used email address and cell phone if they are willing. Now you have contact info to follow up with them after the event and let them know about future events.

The people who should be the most engaged in this contest are the people hosting the event. In fact, sometimes it may be appropriate to only allow people from the Student Government, Student Activities Counsel, (or whatever organization is putting on the event) to be involved in the contest; after all, there are privileges to having to endure all those long meetings, annoying people and the person who NEVER DOES ANYTHING :). This group should be the most passionate people about the event, therefore they should be bringing the most people!

People like to be involved in something that they can WIN/be a winner. This is why after the hit NBC show *The Biggest Loser* became one of people's favorites, companies all over started hosting their own Biggest Loser competitions within their organization. It was a fun thing they could do to inspire people to lose weight and become more healthy. It is the same with your event! The contest creates a buzz!

TIP #5:

Use Social Media to Build Social Proof!!!

Almost 98% of your students are on one or more of the major outlets of social media (Facebook, LinkedIn, Twitter, Google Plus, Instagram, etc). Plus 96% of students possess some sort of mobile device that they use to engage in social media. It has never been easier to market to people! You can literally, for FREE, send marketing information to someone's hand! You must use social networking as a means of announcement, interest building, emotional marketing (giving them a reason to come - we will go over this later), etc.

If that many students are engaged with social media then that is where we need to be. There is a saying in marketing, "Instead of fishing with a hook, fish with a net." This is the idea that you use marketing that hits as many people as you can with one marketing effort. I would also add to that, you must be casting the net in a lake that has fish! If you go down to the nursing home and market your college student event, I don't care how creative your marketing is, it will be ineffective! That is why social media marketing is so effective - so many people you are trying to reach are there.

Here is the draw back to using social media. Because in most cases you cannot just post, tweet, pin or text something and have your entire campus see it, you will have to do it in a way that people can view your event info. For example, market on your college's Facebook page and get students to like the page so you utilize that for marketing purposes…OR build a group on any of the social networking sites and start marketing that site!

Social media is never THE marketing tactic; it is simply one of many!!!! Often times because I can sit behind a computer or phone, this type of marketing is easier and takes precedence over other methods! This is *another* method, not the *primary* method.

TIP #6:

Get the Best!!!

One of the best ways to get people to your event is to hire a speaker, comedian or musical artist that your students would find fun, interesting and enjoyable! One of the most attractive things to college students is humor and entertainment. Now, if you are a student leader, or student coordinator, I know what you are thinking (I know that sounds a little creepy...but hey, that's my gift): "Yeah but if I am seeking to get content, I don't just want someone up there telling jokes; our students need life-changing content." Let me dispel a myth: most people think when humor is present content is absent. This may be true of some speakers, however your job is to find the ones who do an exceptional job at joining the two together. Great speakers use humor to break down social barriers and build rapport with their audience so that when they teach the life changing content they have the audience's attention. We have proven over and over again that people learn way more when they are laughing. This is why many people remember jokes that a comedian told, but don't remember the facts of science class

Humor is, in fact, the best vehicle to deliver content. Studies show that when people are laughing they learn, internalize and implement more. They make a positive association to the content. Believe me, one of the sure fire ways to kill the attendance of your events is to hire speakers who are the same old motivational or leadership speaker up saying "Go - get em!" You need people who are different and communicate in memorable ways.

When students believe they are going to have a good time, they are much more likely to give up their precious time to come to something "extra". Let's remember to convince them that they can't live without this event. That is why getting an entertaining and humorous speaker is imperative. I have yet to find a topic that humor doesn't make better.

This is why professional comedians can get anywhere from $10-60 (and even more) a ticket to see them perform. People love to laugh. Give them what they want (to laugh and have fun) while giving them what they need (the life changing content). This will leave you, as the coordinator, looking like the hero.

Remember, students will never complain about laughing too much, they will however complain about a speaker who was boring.

Ask the speaker/entertainer for a video so you can get a feel for how they entertain and engage people at the same time!

TIP #7:

Don't Tell...but SELL!!!

Facts tell emotions sell!!! On all of your event marketing material highlight the fun they will have and the benefits they will receive. For example, which of the following statements are more compelling?

1. *"When:* Tuesday October 14. *Where:* Columbia Hall. *What:* The Greatest Leadership Event Ever. *Who:* Mike Fritz is our speaker. *Why:* Because we desire all of our students be to leaders. Most students can accomplish more than they are. This seminar changes all of that! Make sure you are there.

OR:

2. Tuesday night, October 14th we have put together an event to get you away from the books, out of the libraries and away from everyday stress. If you come to Columbia Hall at 8:00pm we are offering

you a 60 minute vacation, filled with food and fun. Mike Fritz is going to make you laugh until it hurts, and inspire you to "Make Leadership F.U.N." giving you the tools you need to positively impact hurting people around you. There are people on our campus right now who are limping through life and your skills and talents are the answer to their problem. In fact, the first 50 to the event get a FREE copy of Mike's book "Great Student Leader's Aren't Born They're Made." Be there - you DESERVE a break, and our campus needs YOU!

LET'S BREAK DOWN WHY I WORDED THE SECOND ONE THE WAY I DID:

1. You see how the second one appealed to the emotional desires of college students. There isn't a college student out there who doesn't desire a break to do some laughing!

2. I call it a vacation. I do this because for most people vacation brings back great memories, other than for some who took the whole family, extended relatives and everything to Hawaii or something, and then you are just crazy!!! Use language that connects with positive emotions in their mind.

3. Instead of just saying Mike Fritz, I said, "Mike will make you laugh until it hurts and inspire you to Make Leadership F.U.N." This is marketing. Especially if I am speaking some place for the first time and the people don't know me as well - then that is even more important.

4. I used the phrase "...positively impact hurting people..." Most people have hurting friends or family they want to help but don't know how. After they leave this session they are going to be able to be the change agent for all of that - that is very inspiring. You will of course have to tweak this to fit your particular event.

5. I mention, "There are people on our campus right now who are limping through life and your skills and talents are the answer to their problem." I brag about the people I want to come before I tell them (I don't ask them - I'll tell you why in a minute) to come to the event. I have served them first. I have put them in a good state of mind before I ask them for things.

6. I use the "Bonus Technique." The first 50 who come get a free book. Give them an incentive to come.

7. I mention, "You deserve a break..." I call this "playing into their perceived rights." Most people believe they work so hard they deserve a break

- so agree with them and offer them not only the break they need, but the break they WANT!!!

WHEN YOU ARE MARKETING THE EVENT THERE ARE A FEW WORDS THAT YOU NEVER USE (ESPECIALLY WHEN YOU HAVE A LECTURE-TYPE SPEAKER).

1. *"Seminar"* - this says you will "learn" something while "event" says I will experience something.

2. *"Learn"* - students are sick of "learning" things; they "learn" things all day long...they want to come and have fun!

3. *"Training"* - much for the same reason you don't use the word "seminar." People are sick of being trained - we are not dogs people!

4. *"All day"* - even if the event is an "all day" event, it emphasizes the duration rather than the benefit!!!

5. *"Teach"* - once again, students are sick of being taught...they are in class all day. Replace with words like "inspire", "motivate", "move", "energize", etc.

TIP #8:

The 3 V's of Event Marketing!!!

When marketing your events you must use the cheap forms of marketing at your disposal, especially if you are on a limited budget - which most events are! There are 3 forms of marketing that you MUST use! In fact, if you neglect one or more of these then your event will suffer at some unknown level!

THE 3 V'S OF SUCCESSFUL EVENT MARKETING!!!

Vocal Marketing: This type of marketing is the least amount of money and often the most effective. Vocal marketing is the effort to talk to as many people as you can about the event! Have you ever heard somebody say, "What's all the buzz about?" The reason they say that is because people are talking about something that they have caught wind of. This is the goal of vocal marketing.

What I like to do is enlist 10 "Vocal Advocates." These are people who possess the job of talking to 10 people a day about the event who might be able to come (what I mean by this is that you are not talking to people who are not from your school if it is a school-only event). That means that 100 people a day are hearing about your event. You can imagine how this spiderwebs. If we start marketing 4 weeks before the event, that means that 2,800 people have heard about it; and that is not even counting the people who have heard about it and talked to their friends! This is very effective.

Visual Marketing: People remember what they see over and over again. Often times visual marketing is not a direct sale, but one where you are simply implanting images into their subconscious about the event. For example, when you go to a hockey game, what do you see all around the boards on the inside of the rink; or what do you see around the outfield of a baseball field, or what do you see driving down the road, or on placemats at some restaurants? You see advertising. The reason restaurants do this is because you are watching the game and not thinking about the advertising. This is the best time to advertise to you. Why? Because "the walls" of your subconscious are down and those images get implanted into your mind. Your conscious mind always goes to your subconscious mind to make decisions. So when you leave the game and you are "all of a sudden" craving a Big Mac from McDonalds, there is a reason why. You were just advertised to for 3 hours without your knowing it. When you do this on your campus you are implanting images of your events in the minds of the students on campus. This is so powerful.

People are exposed to anywhere from 5,000-20,000 pieces of advertising a day. But here is the thing; very rarely do people see a billboard advertising an upcoming movie and call the theater right away because they saw the billboard. It goes the same with the other examples above. If that is true then why do very successful companies market this way. They are seeking to get in front of you one more time because, in marketing, it takes at least 5-7 exposures for a person to buy. Think about this in relationship to your event. People need to have 5-7 exposures to the promotion of your event before they will come. However, if the are told about the event or invited to the event by a friend the number decreases drastically; that is why verbal/vocal marketing is so effective.

Virtual Marketing: I think I can say with some level of certainty, the internet is here to stay! It is said in business that if a person's website is down it is like their doors are closed! Many people believe that if it's not online it's not credible! You must have your events accessible online! This means that you are adding it to your organization's website and all forms of social media including YouTube, Vimeo and others if you don't consider those "social."

Most colleges have a fan page on Facebook because other people do, and they seek to get "Likes" because they perceive that is better! The ONLY reason you seek to get likes is to open and continue a conversation with the people who follow, like or subscribe to you. As far as events go, one of the main reasons I think people need fan pages is so you can continue to market to people who have already attended your event and to those who support what you are already doing. PS - at every event make sure you announce to go to your social media and "like" your page so you can continue to keep them updated in the future.

Never...never...never have an event with out doing a promotional video! Why? Video connects with people and people think in images! Some days YouTube beats google as the most used search engine in the world! Video is SO powerful!!! Make a video with your team that is fun, funny and engaging and send it to everyone's page you know!!! You must use the internet!

TIP #9:

Market to the "Wanters" not the "Needers"!!!

It is a huge marketing mistake for your event to market to the people who "need" your event! You might be thinking, "What in the heck is this guy talking about?" What I mean is, it doesn't matter how much people need your event - and I am sure they do - if they don't WANT your event, they won't come!!!

When putting on an event ask your team "Who is the most likely person who would want the type of event we are promoting?" If we are bringing in a classical band, you might think about marketing to all your music students. If you are having a leadership speaker, you might talk to all the organizational members (Student Government, Student Activities, Student Life, Greek Life Leaders, etc). If you are having a spoken word poet, you might offer to artists, both musical and physical, as well as english majors, etc.

I totally understand that there are many people who "need" your events, however they may not want them! That is okay - that doesn't mean you are not putting on relevant events or that your event isn't a world-changing event; all it means is that there are people who want your stuff more than others. In fact, your event attendance will increase when you focus your marketing to the people who want it - EXCLUSIVELY. The greatest mistake marketers make is creating a product, or in our case an event, and THEN going and trying to find someone who wants it. Find out what they want ahead of time and give it to them.

You may have to do a survey on campus and ask students what types of events they would actually attend. This helps you understand your campus better as well as informs your marketing process. You see depending on the type of person you are targeting for your events your language, titles, colors, decorations and maybe even the location will change. With each event you want to get to know the people you are targeting.

Make it your quest to find and market to the people who want the type of event you are offering. Then let the people who want it invite people who may not want it, but will come because their friend is going. This is thinking like a successful event marketer!

TIP #10:

Social Proof is TRUE no Matter if it's False!!!

Every time you have an event you need to become a TM (not testosterone machine people!). This stands for Testimonial Machine. Every event you have, you should be collecting testimonials from the people who attended so you can use them on your marketing in the future. If you are part of a Student Government Association imagine if you gather this testimonial from another student:

"I attended the SGA event and it was awesome. I will definitely be looking for their next event to make sure I don't miss it." - Sara, Freshman

This builds social proof without you being the one saying it. Often if you say something about yourself people may not trust it … but when others say it, it is trusted immediately because the people reading it assume the person has no reason to lie about it (and in almost all cases they are right). Social proof is one of the most powerful tools in your marketing that you could ever use.

You want to get testimonials from people who are "JUST LIKE" the people you are marketing to. The reason for this is people will listen to people who are just like them much faster than someone they perceive is different. If you got a testimonial from a professor about your event it would not have nearly the impact as if you collected a bunch of testimonials from other students (assuming your event is for students).

Every event you have, collect testimonials of its attendees. You could possibly give people a free book, CD, or other gift if they are willing to give a positive statement about your event! You need to get as many as possible because you won't use most of them. You are collecting 100 to be able to use 10. Always… Always… ALWAYS collect testimonials after EVERY event!!!

Here is where this tip becomes magical. Make a list of reasons why people wouldn't attend your event: maybe it is time, or they don't know anyone else who is going, or it doesn't sound fun, or, if it is a paid event, they don't have the money, etc. After you have your top 3-5 reasons you seek to find testimonials that address the reasons why people wouldn't come. Your testimonials are meant to alleviate reasons why people wouldn't come with testimonials from people just like the people you want to come.

IT WOULD LOOK AS FOLLOWS:

- If you are seeking to address the issue of students being too busy, you seek to get a testimonial that sounds something like this:

  "I am so busy… and almost didn't come because I have so little time, but I am so glad I did. This was worth the time… believe me you should come to the next event." -Sara, 2nd Year Student

- If you are seeking to address the issue of not knowing anyone else who is going, you would seek to get a testimonial that sounds something like this:

  "I didn't know anyone else who was going, and because of that, almost didn't go myself. But I am so glad I did… I met so many cool new people." - Sarah Smith, Sophomore, Elementary Ed Major

IF YOU ARE HAVING A PAID EVENT, YOU MIGHT SEEK OUT A TESTIMONIAL THAT SOUNDS SOMETHING LIKE THIS:

- "I really didn't have the money to come, but I am so glad I made it happen. This was so worth the money and I would do it again in a heart beat." John Franks, Junior, Communications Major

  You may be thinking, "Yeah but how do you get testimonials that are so specific?" The short answer is, you ask for them and you give ethical bribes for them. After each event you say this, "We are giving away coupons for a free pizza to "Local Pizza Shop" for anyone who would give us a few positive comments about the event to let others know how much fun we had." Then when people are lining up to give you testimonials you tell people what kind of testimonials you need. You may say, "Would you say something about how the cost was worth it and people should find a way to come no matter what?" This way you are manufacturing the type of testimonials that will help you remove objections from the people you want to attend.

After you get these, you start using them on every poster, Facebook announcement, website and flyer that you can.

TIP #11:

Make T-Shirts for Your Event With the Event Details on the Back and Have People Sit in the Front Row!!!

This trick is helpful for, yet another, visual exposure and then gets represented in many classes throughout the day by multiple students. People begin asking "What is up with the orange t-shirts?" (or whatever color you choose)

When implementing this tip you want to use bright, beaming colors. Bright orange, bright yellow, neon green, etc. These are colors that would stick out in the front of a classroom and around campus.

This tip does take a few dollars to pull off. You can get shirts printed for about $6 per shirt most of the time depending on how many you print, so it may cost you $100 or so to get shirts for your organizational members.

A bonus to this idea is to ask the professor if you could announce the event right before class. You might say, "You may wonder why we are wearing orange T-shirts today. It is because we are having a Leadership experience this week that will blow your mind. We are going to have a celebrity speaker, food, hangout time…it is going to be amazing. It is this Friday and Saturday. Make sure you are there. In fact, I have the details on the back of my shirt." Then sit down and you have told them to stare at your shirt without telling them to stare at your shirt.

TIP #12:

Write it on the White Board When You Go to Class so People See it When They Come in and Sit Down

(YOU WILL OBVIOUSLY HAVE TO ASK THE PROFESSOR IF THIS IS OKAY)!!!

You will have to clear this by the professor teaching the class, but usually, because it doesn't take time out of class they are okay with it.

When you do this, you write "Free Comedy Night" or "Free Date Night" or "Sex...Now That I Have Your Attention..." in big black letters. The reason for this is that students know and have been trained to read "announcements" ever since they were in grade school. What happens is many of the students may think it is announcements for this class so they will be sure to glance at them. This is great exposure for your events!

When writing on the board make sure you lead with the benefit and then invite them to come. It is always great to start out with a question. It may sound like this:

"STRESSED AND TIRED???? Come Laugh Friday with FREE Dinner"

It doesn't have to be word for word … but something like this is VERY effective.

Also right after class, write it again so that the people leaving class see you writing something and may stick around to see what, plus the next class coming in may see it as well.

TIP #13:

Market to a Captive Audience!!!

Where on your campus do students have to stay in one location for a few moments that may give them a second to read your poster. For example: back of bathroom stall doors (they aren't going anywhere), above urinals in the men's room, on the back of elevator doors, on the wall where people stand in line, in the food court to get food, etc. The idea is to place your marking where they will be for a few seconds and not move.

Your goal with this type of marketing is to simply get them to see it one more time! You might even think about having a creative name for this type of marketing.

I was speaking at a college recently in NYC and this particular campus marketed in the restrooms regularly. They called their marketing pieces "The Stall Street

Journal." What a great way to get people to remember and read your stuff.

How about adding a joke of the week, or some type of humor on your marketing piece? People will get used to a joke and will read it every time they go in just to see what the new joke is. Make it fun and funny and people are much more likely to remember it!

Did you ever get on an elevator with someone you don't know; isn't that the longest 15 seconds of your life? People are dying for something to look at, read, etc. That is one of the reasons many times people are on their phones in elevators.

Put your poster on the back of the door and give people something to break that crazy, awkward moment with.

Another trick to use after you have hung your posters on the back of elevators when you personally are on the elevator with someone, talk about the poster. Say something like "Are you going to that? I think I am…it looks fun." Then get off the elevator. Again, this is social proof.

TIP #14:

Market with Placemats

Locate students in your college's design center and have them design a piece of marketing that looks like a placemat with all of your event details on it. Then place them where the students are going to eat.

The power in this technique is students are staring at it for quite a while rather than simply walking by a poster. They may read it 2 or 3 times. This again, is another example of marketing to a captive audience.

In the right corner of the placemat write, "Please leave this mat for the next person. Thank you so much." This way you don't have to print as many and you can collect them after each day and place them out before lunch. You will have to locate who is going to be responsible for dropping them off and picking them up.

Make sure you identify someone on your team to go and set them out and pick them up, and throw out the ones that are trashed at the beginning and the end of lunch.

Again, it isn't that this is the magic bullet, but just another way to get your event in front of people.

TIP #15:

Film a Video for Every Event!!!

Videos are powerful! You want to make sure you leverage them for each of your events. If you are a campus that does a few events a week you may have to choose a few events a month that are your "bigger" events. The point is, you want to start promoting your events with videos and start placing them on all forms of social media your campus uses, as well as sending a link to everyone's campus email. You may say, "Yeah, but no one looks at their email." Your goal isn't to get it to the people who don't, but rather the few people who do are now exposed to your event. Remember, one form of marketing is never the golden ticket, but rather, success is when you do as many forms of marketing as possible.

HERE IS A SUCCESSFUL VIDEO IDEA...

Go around campus, with snickers bars and ask people if you can interview them for a FREE candy bar. The point of the interview is to promote your event. So if you are having a leadership speaker, you would ask people what they believe leadership is. If you are having a comedian, you would go around and ask people who there favorite comedian is and why OR ask them to tell their favorite joke and then make a reel of jokes that are probably not that good and make a video that states... "You want some REAL jokes? Come and see comedian Mike Fritz."

The point of an interview video is to engage students who are just like the students you will be marketing to; remember you want to target the students who are most likely to come to your event. It not only lets the people you are interviewing know about the event, but gets them talking about it to their peers, friends and others.

Let them know that the video will be played at the event so they won't want to miss seeing their interview played in front of the entire audience. This, again, gives them a reason to come and invite their friends.

What does the Liberty Tax organization, the "We buy Gold" business and Little Caesars have in common? They all use the tactic of having a guy in a costume out on the corner twirling an arrow, dressed up like pizza, etc. to draw attention and thus get business. So what you can take from this is, while you are doing the interviews, have a person who follows the camera around carry a big sign, maybe even dressed up, to draw attention to your event. Then hand out flyers and invite people to come or even ask others if they would be willing to be interviewed.

This tip takes a bit of planning but can be very effective and FUN for your group to do together!

Book Mike to speak on your campus at www.mikefritz.net

TIP #16:

Market The Benefits NOT the Event!!!

This is one of the biggest mistakes of campus marketing. Students put on great events and market the events. You may say, "Yeah, but isn't that the point?" You ALWAYS want to market the <u>benefits</u> of the event not the event itself. There is a MASSIVE difference and often the difference of whether people will come or not! Let me explain!

If I wanted to buy a Ferrari (which I ABSOLUTELY do) when I go to the dealership, the salesman is not going to sell me based on the car itself. For example, if they explain to me the high quality paint, the awesome tires and the horse power of the engine, nothing inside of me will think, "I can't live without that car." Why? Because none of those are reasons why I want a Ferrari. IF you want to sell me on getting a Ferrari, tell me how I am going to look in the car. The status that I am going to achieve among my peers, how everyone is going to want to be me, how I will turn heads at every stop light and so on. All of those are benefits of having the car, not the car itself. You have to help people see the benefits of attending your events.

Every morning people wake up and tune into WIIFM Radio - "What's In It For Me?" So for every event you put on, your marketing should have the answer to that question. You have to sell them on what "benefit" they are going to get by attending. If you are following this you should be asking yourself, "Yeah but how do you determine the benefit of the event that you are marketing?"

This is a great question! You find out the benefit by defining the pain that your event relieves or the problem your event solves. If you are putting on a comedy night you are alleviating the pain of being stressed out with homework, work and the overall stress of life. If you are throwing a welcome week for freshman, you are alleviating the pain of not knowing anyone and sitting home alone while everyone else is having a blast. If you are throwing a leadership event, you are alleviating the pain of feeling like your life doesn't matter and no one would miss your presence if you were gone. If you are throwing a night with a magician, hypnotist or musician, you are alleviating the pain of wanting to do those things but not having the money to experience them. You see how every event alleviates some sort of pain?

So after you have defined the pain you eliminate, then you also state it in the positive on your marketing. You alleviate the pain of being stressed out and being trapped in the library when you have a comedian, but also state it in the positive: "This Saturday let us get you away from the books, out of the dorm (this is the pain) and let us give you a 60 minute vacation where you will get free food, great people and a night you won't forget" (this is stating the same thing positively).

I say, "You always have to POP your marketing." POP stands for "Pile on Pain." You have to, through the images and words you use on your promotional materials, help people physically feel the pain of NOT coming to your event so they do indeed come and don't miss out!

You have to pile on the pain, then explain the benefit and then, most importantly, *ask them to come*. Most people miss this last step because they assume the fact that they are marketing and people are reading it, that people want them to come. The greatest mistake of any salesman is not asking for the sale. You have to ask them to come and enjoy this night with you!

"People don't buy products…they buy the benefit of what products give them."
- MIKE FRITZ

TIP #17:

Choose the Right Day and Time for the Audience You are Marketing to!!!

Review tip #9 before reading this tip. The point of picking the right time is making it as easy as possible for your target audience to attend. There are many reasons why people don't attend campus events, and the time of the event is often near the top.

For example, if you choose to have events at a time when the majority of your campus is in classes this will for sure be a shot to the attendance of your events. Another sure fire way to kill the attendance of your events for college students is to have them early in the morning. Many college students are up late, so to have something early in the morning is a hurdle most students have to get over in their minds to get themselves out of bed and show up. I know you may be saying, "Yeah, but if we are having a leadership event (for example) we should be willing to get up early, after all, we are leaders." While I agree, there is no reason to place that obstacle in front of people if you don't have to.

With that being said, I have spoken at many leadership conference that started at 9am and so on. First of all, these events are almost always on Saturdays and they are RSVP events. Early mornings can work for conferences where people will be engaged for the majority of the day. This works because people see the benefit of a conference over an event. IF you are going to get up for a one hour event, your mind automatically says, "It's not that big of a deal if I miss it." If it is an all day experience, your mind says it is worth the investment because there is a lot of benefit to be had (as compared to one hour). Now, not everyone will be thinking this, but for leadership training (or something similar) your target audience would be more likely to do this.

You must survey your campus to see what times work best for events. I have spoken at colleges where every Wednesday they have 2 hours off in the middle of the day and the campus uses that time for events. Or, if it is a resident campus (where students live on campus), evening events work very well. If it is a commuter campus, getting people to come back at night can be difficult, but if you sell the benefit strong enough this can work. If you are a commuter campus and you ask people to come back at night, always offer dinner (and child care if a high percentage of your students have children!).

Time of events is one of the most important parts of planning. Make sure the times you choose make it as easy as possible for students to say "Yes" to attending your events!

TIP #18:

Market in 21 Day Cycles!!!

Things told too far in advance are often forgotten. It is easy to think that by marketing far in advance you have a better chance at boosting attendance. This is often not the case though. The people who do end up attending make the choice a few weeks, and often a few days before your events.

If I tell you that we have something going on next month, even if next month is 4 days away, your mind automatically places it to the back burner because it thinks it has loads of time to make the decision whether to attend or not. If you market in 21 day cycles you stand a much better chance of marketing within people's window of decision making.

This will mean you must have a marketing calendar. You layout out your calendar so you are marketing 21 days before the date of each event. When I say, "It is just 20 days away...you need to reserve your seat NOW!" vs.

"Next month we are having (fill in event). Sign up right away." The urgency is removed because my mind believes it can make the decision later.

Many organizations do one event per week. So each week you will be marketing anywhere from 2-3 events. This will take a lot of planning and organization, but it is these types of things that take your events to the next level.

Our brains are often programed in 21 day blocks. There is a reason it takes 21 days to form and break a habit. Let's use this to our advantage and start marketing in time frames that make it easy for students to remember the dates of your events.

TIP #19:

Event to Event Marketing!!!

Every event you have is the greatest. Think about your next event. You have worked hard to promote it thoroughly and get students to attend; you have made sure all of the necessary elects were in place to have a killer event; you have invited the best speaker or entertainer you could find and the event is a huge success. You have worked so hard to get people to this event, however if you don't market your next event while you have these people here, you have missed a huge and easy opportunity.

This is called event to event marketing. Every time you have an event you have flyers, post cards, announcements and marketing on the screen when people come in explaining your next event. I speak at campuses all over the country and rarely do I see organizations marketing their next event at the event in which I am speaking. You want to capitalize on the events you have already worked on to help your upcoming events. It is easy and very cheap to mention another event while this event is going on!

The first mistake is to not mention your next event at all; the next mistake is to mention it in a low energy, boring way done by someone who is a bad public speaker. This will give your next event bad PR and will likely end up with the people who you tell not coming. You want this to be done in a fun way. Maybe do a skit that is hilarious, done by your drama department (of course you need to plan and organize this). You want this to be done well and represent your next event in a captivating way.

Think of the next event coming up for you. How can you make sure everyone who attends is made aware of any other upcoming events you have?

TIP #20:

Blitz Marketing!!!

This tip is quite possibly one of the most effective and practical tips on boosting event attendance that you will find in this book. Blitz marketing is a phrase I have coined that means for 2 hours before your event you send out people to go get more people to come to your event. Let me explain…

I said earlier that we think in 21 day cycles. While this is true, people often make final decisions on the spot and last minute. I say, let's use this to our advantage! Here is how this works…

You and your team shows up 2 hours before the event. You go out in groups of 2-3 people and walk around campus and ask people if they have anything going in the next few hours. It may sound something like this, "Hey there…we are from the SGA organization and we have a comedian coming in tonight; we are just walking around and letting people know that there will be free food, prizes and a great time. Would you like to go?" If they say yes you ask them, "Do you know anyone else you could call and/or text to let them know so they don't miss out as well?" Then if you are able to get their friend to come, you ask their friends the same question, "Do you know anyone else…?"

I have seen this tip alone add anywhere from 5-100 people to an event. It is so powerful because it asks people to make a commitment for the next few hours, not make a commitment for next Tuesday in the evening when they don't even know what will be going on at that point.

This tip takes a little bit of guts, but is extremely effective in boosting last minute attendance. I had a school do this in NYC and they added 30% to each event just by adding implementing this tip!

BONUS TIP #21:

Add a Marketing Chair to Your Board Members

One of the most beneficial things you can do is add a chair person on your organization who organizes the marketing calendar and thinks of creative ways to market. You want to find someone who thinks like a marketer not an organizer. You might say, "But didn't you just say he/she needs to organize?" Yes...but I have seen it work better with a marketer and an assistant so that all the work can get done.

You see the marketer is always thinking of ways to get more people there, the assistant handles the details of printing flyers...the calendar...etc.

Most of the time, believe it or not, really organized people don't make the best visionary people (people who think of new ideas and directions for the organization). You want to give people a chance to shine where they are gifted, and strapping someone who is great at marketing down to making sure all the details are taken care of will stifle their ability to think up great new marketing ideas, and limit their time as well!

So you need two new positions which are specifically aimed at getting people to your events!

10 TIPS FOR CHOOSING THE RIGHT SPEAKER/ ENTERTAINER OR NOVELTY

TIP #1:

Your speaker asked you to do WHAT?

One of the biggest hinderances to your event when picking a speaker, is picking a speaker who is hard to work with. Every once in a while you get a speaker or entertainer who thinks because you invited him/her to speak at your event that you are there to serve them. This couldn't be farther from the truth! Your speaker has been invited there for 3 reasons: to attract people to your event, make people love your event and make you look like the rock star that you are for the hard work you do putting on amazing events. They exist to serve YOU, partner with YOU and help ensure YOUR event is a success!

Be careful because you often don't know that your speakers are hard to work with until it's too late. The tragedy of this is that you may have already spent your budget on this person, leaving you little to INVEST in the RIGHT speaker who would be easier to work with and then maximize your energy to pour into the students. You want to spend your valuable time and energy on the students, not the speaker. Below, I have provided a few ways that may indicate a speaker will be hard to work with BEFORE he/she comes to your event or before you sign a contract.

1. ***There is a slow response time before the event.*** If you request documents, forms, power points, etc. and he/she takes a significant amount of time (over a week; 48 hours is more reasonable) to respond to you. You have to think about it this way, if they have not taken the time to set up a system to make sure their clients are taken care of before the event, they more than likely won't be mindful enough to think about you and the success of your event when they are on your campus speaking.

Remember...the success of your event should be a speaker's/entertainer's first and foremost concern!

2. ***They don't follow directions.*** This may seem like an elementary principle, however, if you have a speaker who is unwilling to listen to your needs and then follow through, most likely, they won't improve as the event approaches. For example if you send a document to a speaker to fill out to send back to you and it's done incorrectly because he/she didn't listen or didn't read the directions, only expect trouble in the future! I understand people

make mistakes and for that we must always leave room, however when this is a pattern you must beware. Remember, patterns reveal priorities!

Remember...the success of your event should be a speaker's first and foremost concern!

3. ***The speaking fee is of greater concern than the event.*** While paying a speaker what he/she is worth is very important, the success of your event is even MORE important. The finances of any event must be discussed with the speaker and the event coordinator, however, questions such as: "What is the makeup of your audience? What would success look like to you for this event? Could you summarize the purpose of this event in one sentence so my talk matches perfectly with your goals? What have previous speakers addressed and was it successful? Would you mind if I stayed after to sign books and hang out with your people to greater expand the impact of my message?" These questions are of even greater importance. You see, when you look at these questions they revealed that the speaker is truly thinking through the success of your event. Too many times money is the only reason people are professional speakers. Don't get me wrong, money is a big part of it, however it is not the most important thing! After the contract is signed, it is done.

Remember...the success of your event should be a speaker's first and foremost concern!

4. **Be aware of unreasonable requests in their contract.** This is important; listen up!! There is a difference in making requests from an event coordinator, and keeping them busy chasing things that makes the speaker's life easier. Here is the best way to differentiate between reasonable and unreasonable requests: Do the requests being made point towards making your event better, or making the speaker's life easier? Hopefully they are the same thing, but at least evaluate if they are. However, some requests may seem unreasonable, but they are for the success of your event... for example, I have in my contract that my mic is to be left on 15 minutes after I speak and that my continuing education materials be by the most used exit. These help the event not just the speaker!

Remember...the success of your event should be a speaker's first and foremost concern! Oh wait...have I said that before?!

5. **Listen carefully to the words speakers use throughout the contract process (getting the details of the contract nailed down and signed).** Usually speakers who are very easy to work with not only verbalize it, but are concerned about thinking of ways to save you time and

make your job easier. If the speakers seem to be more concerned with the details of the rider and making sure they have everything they want, this is usually not a good sign. On the other hand, for much of the planning process, the speaker should be seeking to add more value and benefit to you as the event coordinator.

Speakers who are difficult to work with don't fit into your powerful mission to change the lives of students. You, as the event coordinator, have so much to think about and so many lives to impact; you want to make sure your focus is on the details of event success.

TIP #2:

Make Sure the Talent You Book Helps People Have Fun!

"People never complain about having too much fun!"
- MIKE FRITZ

There is nothing that will kill your event more than some-body with great content, but who is dry and boring. In fact, these types of speakers have added a certain stigma to the seminar, motivation and leadership speakers in America. If someone was to tell you there was a leader-ship seminar at a local business, what would be the first thought that went through your mind? You would most likely perceive it to be dry and boring. The reason this is such an important tip is because when people have fun they tell others and will return to your future events.

This also goes for a band that just sings but isn't enter-taining, a comedian that isn't funny, etc. Once you have done all the marketing work to get people there, make sure they have fun while they are there, or you may not see them at future events.

When students are laughing and having a blast you want them to associate that fun with the event YOU have coordinated. Then the next time they see an event put on by your organization they pay closer attention to your marketing, they tell others about your events and show up when you have events. In essence, you are building "groupies" for your events. The best marketing is people telling others to come and the best way to do that is make sure they have fun while they are there.

This also goes for bands, comedians, novelties, etc. When searching for bands, look for the ones who are the best stage performers and the ones who engage the audience the most/best. Make sure the comedians you look at are not only funny, but fit the style you want for your campus! You see, no matter what type of event you are bringing, make it fun and entertaining...this really connects with people well!

One way you can do this is look for the endorsements/ testimonials/reviews of other schools they have spoken for. What kinds of things are being said. Look for things like "These guys blew us away. Our students had a blast." You want to look for endorsements that are reflective of people having a blast.

"Laughter opens the heart to learning."
- MIKE FRITZ

TIP #3:

RE-Booking = True Success?

> "Booking says good marketer; re-booking says good speaker."
> **- MIKE FRITZ**

> "Remember...you are looking for a great speaker, not a great marketer."
> **- MIKE FRITZ**

It does not impress me, from a speaking, band, comedian or anything in between stand point, when I see someone who has a ton of events on their calendar. All that tells me is they are good marketers. What tells me they are good at what they do is when they are re-booked over and over by the same organization! Why would you have the same entertainer back year after year when there are so many good ones to choose from? The answer is in the question! The truth is, there aren't that many "good" entertainers.

The reason people have me and some of my colleagues back over and over again is because we add value and unforgettable experience to every event!

I, in no way say this to gloat, but my 92% re-booking rate is the most important stat I look at in my business. I have had one organization bring me back 8 times in 2 years. This tells me as a speaker that I am connecting with the audience and I am meeting the needs/desires of the coordinator!

When you are looking to book a potential speaker/band/comedian (or anyone else), ask them how many of the event coordinators they have spoken for have had them back. Then when they give you the number ask for the organization name(s) and call their event coordinator(s). It takes a few phone calls, but it ensures that you are getting a good performer for your events.

Remember, you are seeking to find an effective entertainer not an effective marketer. Just because someone is a good salesman, does not mean they are selling an effective product! The best test of the "product" in our case is how many times colleges are having them back.

"The effectiveness of events is wrapped in the wrapping paper of a great performer/presenter."
- MIKE FRITZ

TIP #4:

Are They an Author (Speaker, Lecturer Specific)

One of the greatest selling points of any speaker is that they have taken time to put their expertise in writing! In our world of information, people see authors as experts. In fact, one of the greatest marketing pieces to get people to attend your events is that you are having an author or speaker, not just a talker! I'll actually show you in the next section how to use this to get even more people to your event … so stay tuned!

Authorship says many different things about a speaker. First, it shows discipline. You want a speaker who has been disciplined enough (take it from someone who has written 3 collegiate best-sellers … writing a book is a lot of work!) to place his material in writing so he can influence the masses rather than just walking in a room and influencing a few. A good friend of mine, James Malinchak, says, "Anyone can write a book, but not anyone can write a book." Most people will never take the time to put their thoughts and expertise in writing so the masses are influenced. But even more than that, a book shows his/her commitment to their message. Writing a book takes time; take it from the author of 5 books, with every project I dove into, I knew that hours and hours of my life would be invested in each project!

"Books show commitment to a message."
- MIKE FRITZ

Let me make a quick disclaimer; just because somebody has their message in a book, does not mean their information is good. But look at the greatest experts in the country and world. Almost all of them are authors or creators of something that helps people (home study courses, training DVDs, etc.) Book equals expert in the majority of audience members' minds. Read these two introductions below and tell me which you think your audience would anticipate learning from more intensely:

"Our next speaker, Joe Stanley, is a well-known expert on the topic of leadership. He's been sought after for leadership consulting, many corporate executive positions and other leadership endeavors simply because of the amazing way he presents and explains leadership. He not only has a humorous and fun way of explaining leadership, but many say he is one of the best leaders they have ever seen. Speaking to over 50,000 people a year, Joe is no stranger to the leadership world … so please give a warm welcome to Mr. Joe Stanley!"

Or…

"Our next speaker, Joe Stanley, is a national speaker and author of the best-selling book "Great Leaders Aren't Born They're Made". His message of leadership is being heard and read all over the world. People from the ages of 15 to 80 are being impacted by Joe's easy-to-implement strategies found in his book and taught around the world. Many people consider Joe to be one of the most practical leadership speakers out there. Speaking to over 50,000 people a year, using humor and fun to entertain, Joe is no stranger to the leadership world and is impacting thousands through his writing and speaking...please give a warm welcome to Mr. Joe Stanley!"

Whether you think the book is good or not is irrelevant. You are seeking to find a speaker who is entertaining, intelligent and has information that people want. Speakers who have written books versus speakers who have not are just on a different level; and take it from a speaker who has written many books and speaks all over the world you want speakers who are authors so that your event is a hit!

TIP #5:

Connection is Key

I was sitting in a college class completing my bachelor's degree when my non-athletic professor sought to use an analogy using baseball. He was trying to illustrate the topic of urgency. So he tried to take us back to a baseball game. He said, "Picture this...you're at a baseball game and it's the bottom of the 9th inning and there are 2 outs. The pitch comes in and it's hit deep to center field. As the center fielder backs up, the clock is ticking down..." If you know anything about baseball you're laughing right now. My professor certainly didn't know baseball very well, because there's no clock in baseball. This illustrates a radically important point when picking a speaker.

You must pick an entertainer who can relate to your people. Remember this:

The reason this is so important is because people will not listen to people they cannot relate to and don't think we really have an understanding of their life. If I'm listening to a speaker who I think has never walked in my shoes, I am much less likely to listen to what they are trying to communicate. Here's the catch though...people also **will** listen to celebrities, even if they haven't "walked in their shoes", simply because they're celebrities!

This is the kind of speaker you are looking for: the speaker who has experience and intellectual overlap; speakers who not only know MORE than your audience, but have been through similar situations as your audience and have had success/victory. Look for some sort of affiliation between the speaker and your people!!!

HERE ARE SOME THINGS TO LOOK FOR:

1. Have they written a book that applies to your college students?

2. Do they have a degree that is congruent with your students' interests?

3. Are college students their primary audience they perform for?

4. Do they have videos that make them the go-to person in your line of work?

5. Do they have testimonials from students and coordinators just like you?

6. Do they aesthetically fit the part? (I know this may seem a bit weird but the truth is, teenagers

have a hard time listening and being motivated by an old guy in a 3-piece suit… unless that old guy is representing the college they want to attend, or something along those lines. Make sure they look like they fit the industry).

7. Does their brand speak to your people?

A key component to the success of your event is finding a speaker who can relate to, challenge and provide hope to your audience. I speak a lot in the College, youth and Christian markets. In all of these markets, I have unique and specific knowledge that others may not! If I am speaking to college students but had never gone to college there is a barrier right off the bat that I need to overcome.

FOR A QUICK EXAMPLE, HERE IS HOW MY AFFILIATIONS WORK:

High School Market:

1. I was once a high school student and learned the things that teachers want them to know.

2. I wrote the book, "Great Teenage Leaders Aren't Born They're Made".

3. I have successfully worked with high school students for over 10 years.

4. I was a high school teacher for 2 years and also coached high school girls volleyball for 2 years.

College Market:

1. I have a bachelor and master degree, with high GPA's in both while maintaining a wonderful marriage relationship and a full time job through-out (I understand school-work-family-life balance).

2. I have written the book, "Great Student Leaders Aren't Born They're Made".

3. The way I dress and look fits college students.

4. I am known and trusted in the college market as the "FUN Leadership Guru".

Christian Market:

1. Both of my degrees are in religious studies.

2. I was a pastor for 7 years and successfully led two ministries.

3. I was a Christian educator for 2 years in a private high school.

4. I wrote the book, "Great Christian Leaders Aren't Born They're Made".

5. I am the producer of the DVD, "Great Christian Leaders Aren't Born They're Made: Student Edition".

That being said, because my specialty is leadership, I have had many different organizations call me to speak to their people on leadership. Principles are transferable, but you need to make sure the speaker can relate to your audience! Don't pick the "I speak on that" person. If you ask certain speakers what their topic is and they say "I speak on anything people need." Then you might say, "Who do you usually speak to?" They will usually respond, "I will speak to anyone who needs a speaker." These are the people to avoid like the Egyptian plagues.

"Your event will be a massive success when you get entertainers who relate to college students."
- MIKE FRITZ

TIP #6:

Your Fee is WHAT????

> "Book the person who will give you the
> most, not charge you the least."
> **- MIKE FRITZ**

Have you ever asked a speaker what they charge, only to fall out of your chair at what their response was? Believe me, I have been there. Before I became a speaker, I coordinated many events and had this happen to me many times. I thought to myself, "They are only speaking. Why are they charging so much?!"

Here is what I learned: the more they charge, the more value they, not only should but often do, offer. When you are looking for a speaker you want to do everything you can to free up your budget so you can get a speaker who will give massive value. And please, NEVER...NEVER... NEVER go with the cheapest speaker/band/comedian! That is a sure fire way to kill your event!

What I began to do was find ways to save money other places so I could put more money into the talent (speaker, band, entertainer, etc). That way I could then offer as much value to the audience as possible. With larger speaking fees, I could usually get the speaker to donate a book for each attendee, and then stay after and sign them as well as take pictures; or maybe they would be willing to stay after and mastermind with your student leaders. This is the difference in throwing an event and creating an experience!

For example, I speak at colleges for free often. What I will do with many campuses is they will buy 500 copies of my book "Great Student Leaders Aren't Born They're Made." My book price is $20 a copy. That is $10,000 for the total purchase. If they take this route, I cut that in half and sell the books for $10 a piece which equals $5,000. Here is where this gets fun. If colleges pick this they can split (or pay the whole thing out of that) the budget with their "continuing education" budget which is meant for buying books. Then after they get the books, they can then sell them on campus and make all their money back and then some depending on how much they sell for. Here is one creative way to get people on your campus for free. Just buy their product.

This is a side note, but important to understand! In many cases, high-fee entertainers think differently about your event than low-fee entertainers do. That may sound harsh, but it is just the fact. An entertainer who is getting

$15,000 to perform thinks far differently than someone who will come to your campus for $1,000. First of all, a $15,000 entertainer has probably been around the industry long enough to know the ins and outs of what a successful event looks like. I do, however, understand that there are some low-fee entertainers out there with a "high-fee mindset"... but they are few and far between. And if they think like a high-fee entertainer, without very much time, they will be one!

When performers charge more, you are at liberty to ask them to provide more. With a high fee, you should expect them to be thinking of ways to add value to your event. But no matter what the fee is, make sure they are worth what they are asking.

HERE ARE 3 QUESTIONS YOU CAN ASK TO SEE IF THEY ARE WORTH WHAT THEY ARE ASKING:

1. By having them, will I be able to get more students involved in the event?

2. By having them, will more students get involved as a whole after they leave?

3. Are they willing to help create an experience by staying after and meeting with students at a late night jam/hang out, etc?

Also, you must remember, sometimes the greatest value cannot be measured monetarily - at least in the short term. For example, what if team morale increased, people started loving their jobs and, in turn, you had a lower turn-over rate? Or because of this morale, people started talking about what a great place it is to work and then when a job opened up the quality of the people applying increased? Or because the students at your college are being taught leadership principles, they are then applying them in their classes and place of work; wouldn't your college start to get a better name in the community? You see, these things are not monetarily measured, but have a long-term impact on the success of your organization/college/church/etc.

"Look at the value they offer, not
just the fee they charge."
- MIKE FRITZ

"Don't be afraid of high fees, but
be terrified of low value!"
- MIKE FRITZ

TIP #7:

What else do they offer???

Any time you are seeking to book someone for one of your events, ask them if they are willing to give you a bonus for booking them. For example, you may ask that they provide you with a book/CD/DVD/T-Shirt for each audience member, or that they do a second event for a slightly discounted price during the same trip, or maybe you ask them to do a "round-table" after the event with your top student leaders; or a late night jam, dinner or hangout .

Remember, they WANT you to book THEM! You are in the driver's seat in the negotiation process. In fact, they may not even market that they offer a bonus, but they certainly may be willing to provide one. Always ask for bonuses... ALWAYS! While you certainly don't want to disrespect the good their message brings to the world, you also want as many bonuses, and thus value, as you can get to impact your group.

If a performer isn't willing to give a bonus, they aren't thinking about serving YOU! Referring to the previous tip, you are way more likely to get bonuses from high-fee entertainers than you are from low-fee entertainers. High-fee speakers are simply working with a larger amount of money, therefore, can donate more of it toward your value rather than their cost.

"You have to A...S...K to G...E...T."
- JACK CANFIELD

TIP #8:

Have You Heard it Through the Grapevine???

What's the word on the street (or should we say, in the industry association meetings) about the speaker you are looking into? What type of testimonials does he/she have? Who/Where are the testimonials from? What are people saying who had him/her speak to their groups? Does he/she have references? Here's what I'm getting at...

"Make sure the speaker has testimonials from people just like YOU and your group! Make sure other coordinators and any event leaders are saying what you would like to say after you have them speak!" - Mike Fritz

Here is why this is so important: the only people who can tell you what you want to know are people who have booked them in the past! That is why it is imperative that you look for testimonials on their brochure and website to see if these testimonials are present!

You want to see two types of testimonials on marketing materials. Testimonials from those who booked them (most important) and testimonials from those in the audience.

Here is another trick you can use to make sure they are the speaker you are looking for. Beware - this one takes a few minutes! Ask them to provide 3 people who they have spoken for in the last month and call those people!

HERE ARE SOME QUESTIONS TO ASK:

1. Was he/she easy to work with?

2. Were they concerned about adding value or did you have to pull value out of them?

3. What was their conduct like after the speaking time was over? Did they stay after, bolt out the door, talk to people, etc?

4. Was the money you paid equal to the value they provided?

5. Would you book them again next year for this event? Why or why not?

The reason I have provided the questions above for you, is because they cut through the "he/she did a great job" garbage and get to the information you really want to know! You don't want a speaker who "does a good job". You want a speaker who was so good they make your decision of "if you should book them next year" for you based upon their performance and value!

Your overall goal (which we will talk about a bit more in the next section) is to create an event so impactful that people don't want to leave and desire to come back next time! In seeking to do this, you must book the right speaker.

TIP #9:

Home Depot or Contractor???

Home Depot has made a fortune helping the do-it-yourself-er take care of things around the house. In fact, years ago they coined the phrase, "You can do it, we can help." They wanted to specialize in helping the home-owner do repairs and save money without having to hire a professional.

That being said, I used to own a contracting business and I can tell you that most professionals didn't buy their housing supplies from Home Depot. This is because at Home Depot, you save on the product, due in part because the knowledge of the people assisting you is, in most cases, limited at best! Why do you think you save money going to Home Depot? Besides their large volume of sales, it is partially because they don't have professionals working there! Just incase someone is reading this and works at Home Depot, there are a few people there who know quite a bit about home repair. If you are reading this...you are DEFINITELY that kind of person...phew...I dodged that one :)! As a professional contractor, I used professional lumber yards, architects, had my own direct window and door manufacturer, and so on. Why? Because I wasn't fixing my deck on the weekend, I was running a professional business that "Made People's Houses Homes" (this was my tagline). You see the difference!

There is a big difference between the pros and the amateurs in just about every area of life. You want to make sure that the speaker you choose both presents themselves as such and is truly a professional. There are a number of things, which I will list a few in a moments, the pros do and think about that amateurs do not!

THERE ARE A FEW WAYS TO TELL IF THEY ARE A PRO!

1. *Find their video and watch them.* Are they the kind of speaker who will "wow" your crowd?

2. *Look at their brochure and website.* Are there pictures of them speaking to large crowds? Have they written a book or produced a CD or DVD? You can tell a pro from an amateur often by looking at the quality of their marketing. Are they carrying around a little, tri-fold brochure that they got from vista print or are they using a

professional piece of hard mail (if they use that type of marketing)?

3. *Look at their website.* What do you see? Radio affiliations? TV affiliations? Endorsements/testimonials from other celebrities and professionals?

4. *Are they self-represented or are they working with an agency or management company?* You want speakers who are represented. They are, often times...simply better! Now, there are some speakers who have turned down agencies that want to work with them, however most speakers don't mind having others out there getting gigs for them.

5. *Do they have an email/opt-in list to track* and continue providing people with value?

These are the things professionals do to offer a great product to more people, rather than trying to book a speaking engagement!

"Amateurs speak at your events, pros help
turn your events into experiences!"
- MIKE FRITZ

TIP #10:

Um...can I have my money back???

Why do money-back guarantees make you feel better about the product being offered? Isn't it because you know the company selling the product believes in what they are selling and because they are the only person who can lose by offering a money-back guarantee. It is like a pillow you can lay your head on. In fact, car companies that offer longer warranties usually sell more cars, as long as their prices are competitive. Why? People want the insurance and assurance that what they are buying is going to be up to their "satisfaction."

Never book a speaker who is not willing to give you a 100% money-back guarantee. If they are not willing to stand behind their product, you certainly shouldn't. Often times entertainers who offer it never have people request their money back ... because they are good! I am sure from time to time this happens, but it is extremely rare.

> "If speakers offer you a guarantee, you most likely will never use it; but the speaker who doesn't, after they perform, you may wish they had one!"
> **- MIKE FRITZ**

You certainly would never want to use this unless the contract wasn't met or they promised something and clearly didn't deliver. The reason I say this is for your protection! Entertainers in the industry talk and when an event coordinator asks for money back, you can get a poor reputation fast. I am not saying there isn't a time to ask for your money back, but make sure it was a contractual breech or something along those definitive and objective lines.

The 100% money-back guarantee isn't so you can get your money back, it tells you that the speaker believes whole-heartedly in what they offer. It is something objective that tells you if the speaker believes that what they are offering really meets the needs or and helps people.

I have a friend in the speaking business who teaches students how to get better grades in college. His guarantee is so strong you want to book him just after reading it. He states that if you do what he says and you get less than a B in any class he will give you $100 per class! Now THAT is strong!

I understand that maybe a speaker hasn't thought to put it on their marketing materials, but you must look for it. Once again, just because they don't have a guarantee doesn't mean they are going to fail at your event; however, it can be, yet another, reflection of a pro versus an amateur.

A NOTE FROM MIKE

Often when I speak to student organizations, colleges, retreats, and the like, I am asked to help apply these principles in specific ways. This is why I created my student leadership package for organizations I speak to. Contact me for more information so we can discuss if your organization QUALIFIES for this great value.

When I come to your campus, I not only do a keynote for all of the campus organizational leaders, but I offer a FREE 90-minute consulting session with the organization who brings me in on how to market, promote and expand their events to get at least 25% more people to the next event!

Go to *www.mikefritz.net* to check availability and fill out the booking form. I would love to come to your campus. If you mention that you read this section of the book you are entitled to a 20% discount.

I hope to see you on your campus soon…helping you and your students Make Leadership F.U.N.!

Made in the USA
San Bernardino, CA
12 October 2015